TESTIMONIALS

Jean-Jacques Joris, MA, JD, LPC, Twin Oaks Farm, Cente
Facilitated Counseling and Learning, Longmont, Colorado

Nikki's book is a wonderful collection of simple yet profound mindfulness practices that are as enjoyable to teach as they are to learn. Unlike many mindfulness workbooks, which cause the kids in our lives to roll their eyes and reach for their smartphones, JustBE is an effective invitation to explore the magic of slowing down and the power of curiosity. With her no-nonsense wise and deeply caring approach, Nikki has invented the Swiss Army pocket knife of mindfulness practice, providing you with a tool for every occasion.

David Chernikoff, MDiv, LCSW, Meditation Teacher, Insight Meditation Community of Colorado

Nikki Levine's JustBE Mindfulness Guidebook is just the kind of resource many parents and teach-ers need right now. With the wisdom of a longtime meditation practitioner and the compassion of an experienced mother, Nikki offers a skillful blend of information and experiential exercises that can be applied at home in family life as well as in the classroom. Helping our children develop emotional intelligence at an early age is one way to give them what they need to live healthy, happy and satisfying lives.

Rachel Workman, MD, Children's Hospital Colorado

Nikki Levine has created a joyful guide to the practice of mindfulness for humans of all ages. She demystifies techniques that are so critical for modern times, and that can liberate us from the chaos of a world filled with stimulation and inundation. I've taught many patients who experience anxiety to use the "Handjam" and they've found it to be a reliable tool to derail non-productive thinking. Nikki incorporates her knowledge, experience and humor to create an irresistible invita-tion to use the wisdom found in nature, ancient texts and modern research.

Mary Wallace, Overtown Youth Center, High School Coordinator

I have seen firsthand how the JustBE mindfulness practices can help provide young people with a powerful tool to cope with the stresses of everyday life and beyond. Working with at-risk inner-city youth of various ages, I feel grateful to be able to share mindfulness with them and help them truly understand that peace begins from within.

Nadine Francis, 2nd-grade teacher, inclusion class at Ruth K. Broad Bay Harbor K-8 Center

The JustBE Mindfulness program has helped many of my students who struggle emotionally to settle and stabilize at times when they're feeling sad, angry or frustrated. It has also helped calm students' stress before a test, by teaching them to notice not only what is going on around them and how it affects them, but to turn inward, mindfully breathe and come back to balance.

D'Mychal Norwood, Residential Recreational Programs Administrator, Miami Bridge Youth and Family Services, Inc.

We serve at-risk youth. It's often challenging to change their thoughts and views on dealing with society and their current situations. But I've noticed their resistance to participate begins to fall away once they experience the benefits of mindfulness firsthand. Learning how to JustBE is a healthy outlet for our youth: They learn mindfulness skills that not only help them adapt to our residential program but can be used when they return home, too.

Dr. Maria T. Rodriguez, Principal, Miami Beach Senior High School

JustBE mindfulness practices teach students how to pause, notice what is going on inside of them and around them and release stress. This helps them make better decisions both academically and socially. I highly recommend the JustBE mindfulness program.

JustBE MINDFULNESS GUIDEBOOK

Guided Practices for Parents, Teachers & Counselors to Invite Calm,
Balance and Awareness into a Child's Life (For Ages 7 & Up)

NIKKI LEVINE, MA
Mindfulness Teacher

ISBN 978-1-54396-543-8

Published by Bookbaby, 7905 Route 130, Pennsauken, NJ 08110

Printed in U.S.A.

First Printing, 2019

ACKNOWLEDGEMENTS

My wish for this guidebook is to evoke deeper connections within your own wise heart and mind, and to the big and little beings to whom you are offering these practices.

Thank you, Mom and Dad, for your lifelong unending support.
You both gave me the courage to take paths that helped me understand the essence of how to JustBE.

Zoe and Maya – Thanks for choosing me as your Mother. I love you both to the moon and back.

Sees – you are truly the sister of my heart.

Greggo – my big brother with a heart of gold.

My beloved niece, Brett Gelnovatch, who lovingly created the illustrations in this book.

JuJu – our friendship makes every day more meaningful.

Bardo – my sweet dog and also a daily reminder to honor the in-between.

Much gratitude to Maura Solis for editing the illustrations and JustBE videos.

Thank you to my editor, Jennifer Scruby, for your lighthearted kind advice and dedication.

Thank you Cheryl Arnold for encouraging me to turn JustBE into a book.

Thank you Naropa University and all the professors there who bestowed their embodied wisdom onto me, which created a fire within to share and be of service.

JustBE Glossary

The following words are commonly used in the JustBE guidebook. They're specifically defined to deepen and enhance your understanding of how to JustBE.

Check In – taking a moment to settle, breathe mindfully and give your mind, body and heart a chance to reveal what is true right now.

Compassion – kindness + action.

Emotional Intelligence – increased capacity for self-awareness, self-management and increased emotional literacy, which is an awareness of one's own and others' feelings and needs (Fleet Maull, Upaya Workshop 2018).

Emotional Literacy – the ability to notice what you are thinking/feeling and to be able to name those feelings accurately.

Empathy – a keen sense of what it might feel to walk in someone else's shoes.

Equanimity – relating to change with a quality of balance, stability and flexibility.

Feelings – how we perceive and name sensations in the mind and body (refer to pages 11-14).

Finger Labyrinth – A labyrinth looks similar to a maze. Labyrinths have been used by people all over the world as a way to connect deeper to the earth and themselves, by slowing down and going inward.

Handjam – Each Handjam is a combination of rhythmic tapping of one's fingers while reciting a JustBE intention. Amazingly, synchronizing the two together helps settle one's mind and body.

Intention – Each JustBE practice has an intention or important message that is recited along with the Handjam.

JustBE – practicing mindfulness (awareness) skills as it relates to our thoughts, words and actions, which enhances self-compassion, cultivates empathy, develops emotional intelligence skills and honors our own inherently kind hearts and the hearts of others.

Mandala – circular symmetrical designs that symbolize well-being and can be found in all cultures throughout time.

Mindful Breathing – to consciously bring one's attention to each breath one takes making each exhale longer than the inhale. Over time, this helps one become more focused and aware of what is happening in the moment.

Mindfulness – paying attention to one's thoughts, words, actions and sensations in each moment without judgment.

Mindfulness in Action – weaving mindfulness into everyday interactions.

Mindful Posture – Each JustBE practice starts with getting the body ready to settle in. For example, when seated on a chair, one's feet should be firmly placed on the ground beneath you. Likewise, if one is sitting on the floor on a cushion, legs should be crossed comfortably and spine straight. Tongue on the roof of one's mouth behind the two front teeth and the jaw slightly open and relaxed. Hands rest in a peace ball (refer to illustration on page 3) in one's lap and shoulders rolled back and down. Make each exhale longer than the inhale. Eyes closed or half-closed.

Needs – basic life requirements, including food, water, air and love.

Non-violent Communication (NVC) – a communication method that addresses the needs, thoughts and feelings of others and of ourselves, which leads to greater understanding and harmony.

Pause – to purposely stop and become aware of the space between one's thoughts and feelings.

Peace Ball – how one places one's hands at the beginning of the JustBE practice. This is an important step in coming into the mindfulness posture. To create a peace ball with one's hands, the back of one's left hand is placed onto the palm of the right hand, then touching the tips of the thumbs together (refer to the description on page 3).

Self-awareness – non-judgmental observation of your thoughts, feelings, body sensations, words and actions.

Self-compassion – being kind to oneself by greeting whatever arises with openness and curiosity.

Self-regulation – the ability to calm oneself when activated by using mindfulness skills.

Unmet Needs – basic needs that have not been met or fulfilled.

Introduction

JustBE mindfulness practices empower kids to calm their minds, focus their attention and find their mental and emotional happy place. These 5 to 10-minute mindfulness/awareness practices make the learning path fun and easy. Brilliant for parents, teachers and counselors, each practice teaches a valuable, engaging lesson; together, they help kids develop the foundation for a balanced and joyful life.

Teaching children how to be mindful is a joyful experience, and the benefits come quickly. Once kids learn JustBE skills, it shifts the way they experience life, helping them become more self-aware, focused, calm and kind. Research suggests that mindfulness training also helps kids develop self-regulation, emotional intelligence and self-compassion, and the good news is that it only takes a few minutes a day to get there.

About the Author

After earning a master's degree in Transpersonal Counseling Psychology from Naropa - a contemplative university where mindfulness practices are a central pillar to developing self-awareness - I wanted to put the skills I'd learned into action for kids.

What Does It Mean to JustBE?

Practicing mindfulness (awareness) skills as it relates to our thoughts, words and actions

Enhancing self-compassion and self-regulation

Cultivating empathy

Developing emotional intelligence skills

Honoring our own inherently kind hearts and the hearts of others

The good news is we ALL can learn how to PRACTICE cultivating the qualities of JustBE.

JustBE Instructions for Parents, Teachers, Counselors and Caregivers

How to Begin

Start by choosing a JustBE guided practice (there are twenty-seven in total) to read aloud as a fun and creative way to offer and inspire JustBE-ing. Always do the practice *with* your child or class, so you can co-create a space to JustBE. Mindfully breathe with them. Do the handjam with them, and highlight how they can put mindfulness into action through everyday interactions with others. And at the end, always remember to place your hands over your heart to honor both your heart and those around you. I've found that teaching in this *collaborative* way leaves everyone feeling part of a collective experience. That gives way to knowing that we are all in this together, we affect those around us and that we all matter equally. You are teaching them but you are also learning with them. When you step into offering in this way, your audience will in turn step in more readily to JustBE-ing.

Each guided practice contains five steps, including a movement element to engage the body and heighten awareness of the mind–body connection. (Go to www.mindfulnikki.com/videos for guidance and inspiration.)

Mindfulness

What it is: It is developing insight and expanding awareness of one-self and others.

How to begin: To begin each practice, we come into a mindfulness posture as follows: Tongue on the roof of the mouth.

- Jaw slightly open and relaxed.

- Eyes closed or half-closed (soft gaze a few feet in front of you).

- Hands in lap in a peace ball—place the back of your left hand inside the palm of your right hand, and thumbs touching (refer to the illustration).

PEACE BALL

- Back straight, shoulders rolled back and down, feet flat on the ground if sitting on a chair, sitting toward the edge of your seat. If on a cushion, cross your legs.

- Once settled, guide your audience at the start of *each* JustBE practice through a few gentle mindful movements to help unite the mind with the body and breath. These movements prepare you to begin your JustBE practice.

- Moving slowly, begin to make five big circles with the shoulders backward and then five forward. Slowly, roll the head in a circle three times. Now roll your head in the opposite direction three times. Now place your hands on your knees to prepare for spine rolls. Inhale and push the chest forward, shoulders back, chin to the sky. As you exhale, bring your chin to your chest and round your back; arms become long. Repeat this twice slowly. Place hands back into a peace ball.

Handjam

What it is: It is a combination of rhythmic tapping of your fingers while reciting an intention. (Check out videos of handjams at www.mindfulnikki.com/videos.)

How it's done: Start by using one hand only. It's usually easiest if you use the hand you write with. Place the elbow of that hand on your hip (your side) and bring your palm open, facing you, so you can see it. Begin by tapping your thumb to your pointer finger; then tap your thumb to your middle finger; then tap your thumb to your ring finger and lastly, tap your thumb to your pinky finger. This is called the "handjam!" Use both hands once you get the hang of it. While you tap your fingers, you recite the intention for the JustBE practice you have chosen, such as "Peace begins with me." The intention matches the rhythm of the tapping beautifully. Try it now! Tap your fingers while reciting the intention together aloud five times, and then silently five times.

Wisdom

What it is: It is an opportunity for the *knowledge* in each practice to *grow* into wisdom.

Why it matters: Practicing mindfulness regularly leads us into wiser ways of being, speaking and acting.

By the way, pay attention to what the children say here—mostly listen and reflect. Keeping a journal to capture the reflections of children grades 3 and above can be useful. Or, you can write your REFLECTIONS on pages 103-109. The children can write or draw their reflections; either way, it deepens their experience and your insight into how the practice is affecting them.

Mindfulness in Action

What it is: It is bringing mindfulness into everyday experiences.

Why it matters: This part of the lesson gives kids examples of how they might use mindfulness to make each day better. It also gives them an opportunity to imagine their own examples.

For instance, one teacher told us about a middle-school girl who used to be easily provoked and often got into fights. Once the student learned the JustBE skills and gained self-awareness, the teacher saw her react differently to provocations. She would pause, take a few mindful breaths to calm herself down and walk away. One can see that once children have the tools to make better choices, their lives move in a more positive direction.

> *Tip*: Write down the handjam and the essence of the mindfulness in action for the week and place it in a visible spot in your classroom or home as a reminder to practice.

Honor

What it is: It is a kind, non-verbal way to connect with ourselves and others.

Why it matters: In this final step of the JustBE practice, we take a moment to feel into our own inherently kind hearts, by taking a deep mindful breath while keeping our hands pressed over our hearts. Encourage everyone to honor themselves by nodding their heads down ever so slightly toward their own hearts, honoring their ability to JustBE. Then honor those around you—students, siblings, teachers and/or parents—in the same way. This simple gesture offers a beautiful and powerful way to connect.

BEST PRACTICES

> *Tip*: Dimming the lights and turning on calming music (Carlos Nakai is always a good choice) before you begin your JustBE practice sets the mood just right.

Teachers

Begin each week with one JustBE practice. Start by reading it aloud and do the practice with your class. Encourage students to use the handjam they learned for that week whenever they feel frustrated, bored or anxious. It's especially useful to practice the handjam before taking a test, speaking in front of the class, after lunch when energy levels dip and whenever they need to focus.

Counselors

Use the JustBE guided practices to help kids learn how to self-regulate, emotionally de-escalate and expand their self-awareness. Have them choose a handjam that would serve them and their current issue, or choose one that you think might enhance their understanding of it. Each JustBE practice teaches the child a new skill, the ultimate goal is that in time, with practice, the skill becomes a way of BE-ing.

Parents

The earlier you introduce these practices, the better. Young kids want to do what their parents are doing. Thus, the best way to get your child interested in practicing JustBE-ing is for YOU to practice JustBE-ing. They will see you practice, get curious and want to try it out! Do each JustBE practice with them. This cancels out the usual parent/child dynamic where they are learning from you. You are teaching them, but you are also learning with them by keeping this intention in mind, so you can co-create something quite beautiful.

> *Hint*: Try not to get stuck on them "getting it" completely. The knowledge that what's being offered is within them is what's important. My experience with my own kids has taught me that mindfulness gets into their awareness, even when it looks like it's not. What you are offering will pop out most likely in some unexpected way, maybe even years later. The important thing is to keep the focus on the process and not the outcome. You're building a foundation that they can turn to when they're ready.

Timing

Most of the practices in this book take about 5 to 10 minutes. There's also an abbreviated 2-minute practice (on pages 8-10) that you can do on a daily basis: before a test, after a transition, on the way to school, before bed or anytime kids feel anxious or distracted.

It takes time to settle into moving slowly, resting in stillness and silence and being in the moment. In my experience, it takes about a month for people of any age to feel completely comfortable with learning how to JustBE. Some kids will deflect by laughing, chatting or actively engaging others around them—anything to distract themselves from being present. This is NORMAL, albeit frustrating. But if you use whatever arises as a way to deepen awareness and teach awareness, then these so-called disturbances become part of the learning curve for both you and them. For example, I might say, "Notice if you're giggling, or feel the urge to talk. Maybe you're uncomfortable with this new practice. That's okay and totally normal. Notice when this happens, and practice pausing and bringing awareness back to your breathing and see if this helps you settle."

If you normalize the situation, kids gradually come to see that they're distracting themselves as a self-soothing mechanism—a way to ease discomfort they feel during the practice. In fact, that's a good thing: learning to recognize any distractions and deflections that come up is key to developing mindfulness and self-awareness. Having the ability to pause and focus in the moment strengthens your ability to pause in the future.

At times, I still have grand illusions that when I walk into a classroom, twenty tiny enlightened beings will stare back at me, all eager to follow along, and that when I get home, my two teenage daughters will be meditating, having finished all their homework and cleaned their rooms. This could happen, I suppose, in some parallel universe! But what's important for you, me and the kids to whom we are offering these practices is to maintain a sense of humor, and to be able to sit in the fire of uncertainty with grace and balance. You got this!

THE WORLD NEEDS YOU AND MORE PEOPLE LIKE YOU PRACTICING AND SHARING THIS WAY OF JUST BE-ING.

JustBE
2-MINUTE GUIDED MINDFULNESS PRACTICE

Instructions: Set a timer for 2 minutes. (You can use Insight Timer, a free phone app.) Program it to ring a bell or another sound of your choice at the start and end of the practice.

JustBE mindfulness posture: If you are sitting on a cushion on the ground, cross your legs comfortably. If you are on a chair, sit near the middle or edge of the chair, so that your feet are flat on the ground and your back isn't touching the back of the chair. Bring your spine straight and roll your shoulders back and down. Set your hands in a peace ball. Place your tongue on the roof of your mouth, just behind your two front teeth and keep your jaw slightly open. (This relaxes the neck and facial muscles.) Keep your eyes closed or half-closed, gazing down.

> *Tip*: In time, most people will automatically assume the posture once you say, "Let's get into our JustBE mindfulness posture." Either way, guide them through the steps each time. Some people may laugh or their bodies may be super-jittery. Many are unfamiliar with this kind of "non-doing," so it's always helpful to acknowledge any discomforts that arise. Say something like, "Notice if your body is having a hard time settling, or your thoughts are jumping all over the place. This isn't a problem, but do your best to bring your attention to your breathing. In time, this will become more comfortable, but it may take some practice to get there. Let's practice together." As much as I'd like to say that your audience will sit in silent bliss for 2 minutes, it's probably not going to happen at first. But in time, even the most fidgety or distracted child generally drops into stillness. Even if it's for just a few seconds, it's progress.

Focused breathing: Bring awareness to the sound of your breath, bringing attention to the flow of your breath coming in and going out. Extend the exhale longer than the inhale. This has a calming effect on the mind and body, as it's in the exhale when the body lengthens. When the body lengthens, the mind expands.

Benefits of the practice: It increases focus and attention, enhances awareness of what's going on in the mind, body and heart and strengthens one's ability to pause.

Guided practice: Here's an example of how you might guide your audience through the JustBE 2-minute practice. Sit on a chair or stool if you are in front of a class, so you can do the practice with them. Or if you are with one child, sit beside him or her, so as not to directly face each other. Modeling how to JustBE is the best way to get buy-in, so practice with your audience.

Script

Let's begin our JustBE practice. (Have your timer nearby.)

This is a short time for you to practice JustBE-ing—to take some time out, for a few minutes of "time in." To feel more balanced, it's often helpful to bring awareness to our breath, our body and the ground beneath us.

Let's come into a mindful posture by first straightening our spine—not tight like a statue or collapsed like a rag doll, but somewhere in between. Roll your shoulders back and down, place your tongue on the roof of your mouth behind your front teeth and slightly open your jaw. Let your hands rest in a peace ball in your lap. Keep your eyes closed, or half-closed, gazing down at a point in front of you. It may feel unfamiliar at first to JustBE, but the more we practice it, the more comfortable it becomes. We are almost like scientists, observing what happens as it happens. (This you may have to say only the first few times.)

Begin Timer (Tip: Set a 10-second leeway before it begins.)

As the bell rings, let's begin to bring our awareness and attention to our breath. Make your exhale really long as the sound of the bell fades out. Continue breathing normally, but make the exhale (out-breath) a bit longer than your in-breath. Thoughts are going to come through your mind, and that's normal. Notice them, and then bring your attention back to your breath throughout these 2 minutes. (Pause.) Thoughts are almost like clouds: They are there, you notice them, and then they're gone. Let your thoughts pass through your mind like clouds roll by. Notice them, and come back to focusing on your breath.

When your mind gets distracted, don't judge it as right or wrong, good or bad. Just notice what is happening. Be curious and allow yourself to JustBE. With each exhale, let your body relax even more. (Allow silence now.)

(When there are about 10 seconds left on the timer, let your audience know that the bell is about to ring.) Let the sound of the bell relax you. Remind yourself throughout the day that you have the ability to JustBE.

Slowly open your eyes or lift your gaze if your eyes were half-closed.

Allow the balance we co-created to weave into the rest of your day.

List of feelings when your needs ARE satisfied

© 2005 by Center for Nonviolent Communication

Website: www.cnvc.org Email: cnvc@cnvc.org

Phone: +1-505-244-4041

Directions: Throughout JustBE, use this chart as a way to describe and expand your understanding of feelings when your needs are being met, or when they're not being met.

How to Use: Choose a feeling in bold. The boxes underneath that word help better pinpoint the emotions that are bobbing beneath the surface of your skin and will help you understand what you need. That, in turn, gives you a better chance of getting that need met.

AFFECTIONATE

Compassionate	Friendly	Loving	Open-hearted	Tender	Warm	Sympathetic

ENGAGED

Alert	Curious	Interested	Involved	Stimulated

CONFIDENT

Empowered	Open	Proud	Safe	Secure

EXCITED

Amazed	Dazzled	Eager	Enthusiastic	Lively	Passionate	Surprised	Vibrant

GRATEFUL

Appreciative	Moved	Thankful	Touched

INSPIRED

Amazed	Awed	Wonder

JOYFUL

Amused	Delighted	Happy	Pleased

PEACEFUL

Calm	Clear-headed	Comfortable	Centered	Content	Fulfilled
Relaxed	Satisfied	Serene	Still	Trusting	Quiet

REFRESHED

Enlivened	Rejuvenated	Renewed	Rested	Restored

Feelings when your needs are NOT satisfied

Directions: choose a feeling in bold. The boxes underneath that word help describe and expand your understanding of that feeling when your needs are not met.

AFRAID

Frightened	Mistrustful	Panicked

CONFUSED

Dazed	Hesitant	Lost

EMBARRASSED

Ashamed	Flustered	Self-conscious

TENSE

Anxious	Cranky	Fidgety	Frazzled

List of Needs

© 2005 by Center for Nonviolent Communication

Website: www.cnvc.org Email: cnvc@cnvc.org

Phone: +1-505-244-4041

CONNECTION

Acceptance	Affection	Appreciation	Belonging	Communication	Companionship	Closeness
Community	Consideration	Consistency	Empathy	Inclusion	Love	Respect/ Self-Respect
Safety	Security	Support	To know and be known	To see and be seen	To understand and be understood	Trust

PHYSICAL WELL-BEING

Air	Food	Exercise	Rest/Sleep	Shelter	Water

HONESTY

Authenticity	Integrity	Presence

PLAY

Joy	Humor

PEACE

Ease	Equality	Harmony	Inspiration

AUTONOMY

Choice	Freedom	Independence

MEANING

Awareness	Celebration of life	Challenge	Clarity	Competence	Creativity	Discovery
Understanding	Growth	Hope	Learning	Purpose	Self-expression	To matter

Feeling Faces

(Feeling faces help you recognize what you are feeling and name the feeling)

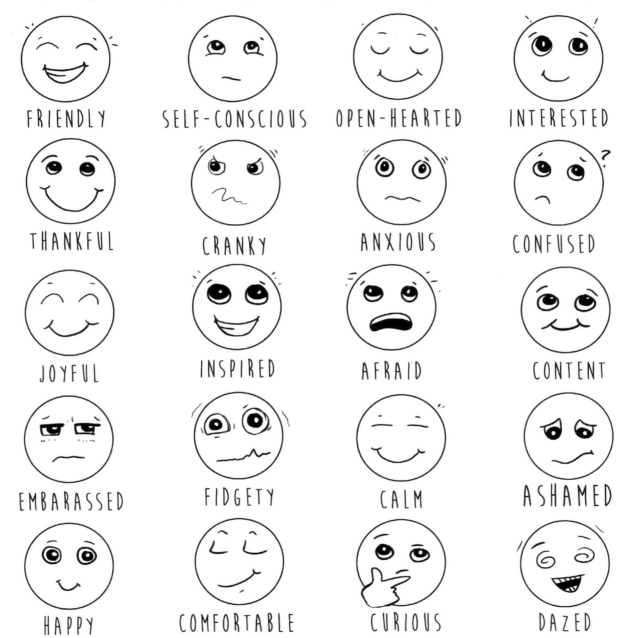

FRIENDLY	SELF-CONSCIOUS	OPEN-HEARTED	INTERESTED
THANKFUL	CRANKY	ANXIOUS	CONFUSED
JOYFUL	INSPIRED	AFRAID	CONTENT
EMBARASSED	FIDGETY	CALM	ASHAMED
HAPPY	COMFORTABLE	CURIOUS	DAZED

OKAY, WE'RE READY TO BEGIN LEARNING THE JUSTBE MINDFULNESS PRACTICES!

(THERE ARE TWENTY-SEVEN IN TOTAL)

I'M EXCITED FOR YOU TO DIRECTLY EXPERIENCE AND DIGEST WHAT IT FEELS TO JUSTBE INSIDE YOUR OWN WISE BEING.

OH, AND HAVE A LITTLE FUN GOING INWARD AND EXPLORING YOU!

1) Peace Begins with Me

Let's begin by getting into our mindfulness posture. Each practice begins by coming into the mindfulness posture and we always take our time at the beginning of each practice to slow down which helps prepare our mind and body to practice JustBE-ing. You may want to refer back to the steps on pages 2 and 3 in the introduction for guidance, until settling into the mindfulness posture and the mindful movements becomes second nature.

The handjam for today is PEACE BEGINS WITH ME.

Mindfulness

At any given moment, lots of thoughts jump through our minds, like monkeys leaping between branches. But sometimes our thoughts can distract us from what's happening right now. The good news is that we can tame those monkeys and learn to work with distracting thoughts. First, sit in silence and just breathe. This will help put the monkeys at ease. Whenever a thought comes into your mind, tell yourself, "breathe," and bring your attention back to your breath. Ok, let's mindfully breathe together for three breaths. Allow your exhale to extend longer than your inhale. This is a practice, so don't get discouraged if you have to say "breathe" many, many times in a short period. That's actually a good thing! You're beginning to train your mind to focus. In time, you'll become familiar with JustBE-ing and have moments where your mind may feel like a monkey that's just hanging out in a tree, napping and calm. Now press the palms of your hands together at your heart center; then rub them together super-fast to the count of 30. Let's count together aloud as we rub our hands. Then release your hands and hold them an inch apart. Can you feel the energy you created between your palms? Take a pause here. Sometimes we need to release some energy to get to a balanced place. Rub your hands together again in the same way as you count to 30.

> *Fun Fact*: When people come together to practice mindfulness, as we do throughout the JustBE program, it doesn't just bring more peace into their own hearts and minds. That peacefulness has a ripple effect, so it serves the world as well!

Handjam

Let's prepare for our handjam. Bring your elbows to your sides (your waist), and let your palms come open. Okay, let's do the handjam together now. Take a deep inhalation and then exhale fully and begin saying the words PEACE BEGINS WITH ME (five times aloud, five times silently) while you tap your fingers. Then place your left hand over your heart and your right hand over your left. Stay here for 10 mindful breaths. Let's mindfully breathe together.

Wisdom

How do we create peace within? The more aware we become of our thoughts, words and actions, the better able we are to choose what we want to say and do, which in turn brings more peace into our lives. The key is practicing mindfulness because it helps you take control of how you respond to what's going on around you. This is your superpower. The JustBE program is specially designed to expand your awareness, so when something difficult arises, you can turn to your JustBE practices and find the skills to be okay from within. Remember, *peace begins with you*.

Mindfulness in Action

Practice finding peace in small moments throughout your day. Whenever you start to feel a little off-balance, take a few mindful breaths or do a few rounds of your handjam and see what changes. See if peace expands within you.

Honor

We take a few moments at the end of each JustBE practice to honor ourselves and one another. With hands placed over our heart (left hand over heart, and right hand on top of the left), together we take a deep mindful breath and honor ourselves by nodding our chin down ever so slightly to our own wise heart and mind. Honor those around you in the same way. If it feels comfortable, look into the eyes of your companions with a soft gaze. Have a mindful day!

WHAT DO YOU LOOK AND FEEL LIKE WHEN YOU REMEMBER TO MINDFULLY BREATHE? DRAW A PICTURE AND/OR DESCRIBE IT IN WORDS.

2) Kindness In, Kindness Out

Let's come into our mindfulness posture. Take your time. Press your feet onto the ground beneath you if you are on a chair. If you're on a cushion, allow your knees to float down and feel yourself connected to the earth. Make small adjustments to your posture, getting your body aligned and ready to practice. Adjust your posture if it feels too tight or too loose.

Today's handjam is KINDNESS IN, KINDNESS OUT.

Mindfulness

Did you know that there are seven billion people living on planet Earth? Pause for a second and think about what might be going on in other parts of the world right now. Those faraway people might look or sound different from us, but they also have full lives just like we do: families, homes, schools, friends and activities. When it comes down to it, we are all human beings who are much more alike than different. Pause and breathe that thought in. Pull your knees into your chest, and rest your forehead down toward your knees, and give your legs a hug. As you rest your forehead on your knees, think for a moment, "How can I offer more kindness to the world?" Take a deep breath and settle into your body. As you exhale, release your legs, and place your feet back on the ground. Imagine breathing out something that will benefit everyone around you. For example, imagine everyone around you right now is receiving kindness from your heart and mind through your exhalation. Imagine this for two more mindful breaths. We will pause often in our JustBE practices. Not to worry, you'll get used to it.

PULL KNEES INTO CHEST

Handjam

Let's prepare for our handjam. Bring elbows to your sides (your waist), and let your palms come open. Take a deep inhalation and then exhale fully and begin saying the words KINDNESS IN, KINDNESS OUT (five times aloud, five times silently) while you tap your fingers. Then place your left hand over your heart and your right hand over your left. Stay here for 10 mindful breaths. Let's mindfully breathe together.

Wisdom

To extend kindness outward, we also must bring kindness into our own minds and bodies. We're taught to be kind to others, which is a great way to be in the world, but we can't forget to be kind to ourselves as well and practice self-compassion. A car needs a full tank of fuel to work properly. Similarly, sending kindness inward is like filling our own tanks, so that we can have enough fuel to offer kindness to others.

Mindfulness in Action

At some point today, choose to pause and take a moment, and as you breathe in, say the word "Kindness" to yourself. As you breathe out, imagine kindness spreading all around you and enveloping the people nearby. Do this for at least three breaths.

Honor

Take a deep mindful breath. With hands placed over your heart (left hand over heart and right hand on top of the left), together we honor ourselves by nodding our chin down ever so slightly to our own wise heart and mind. Honor those around you in the same way. Have a mindful day!

3) Truly Listen

Let's begin by getting into our mindfulness posture. Take your time like you would stacking a set of blocks. For the blocks to remain steady, they need to be balanced just right. Coming into our mindfulness posture requires the same kind of care and presence.

Our handjam for today is TRULY LISTEN.

Mindfulness

Take a few moments to imagine the music made by nature: rain, birds' songs, leaves rustling in the wind, thunder and so on. In a way, life is like a symphony. If you listen carefully, you'll hear noises happening within you and all around you, coming together in perfect harmony. There is a sweet, subtle noise your own breath makes. Close or half-close your eyes, and make a fist with your left hand. Place your fist over your belly button. Place your right hand over your left. Stay here and listen while you take three mindful breaths. What do you notice? What noises are happening around you? Within you? Noticing is the first step in becoming more aware. Don't worry about whether you're doing it right or wrong; just fall into being present without judgment. Your mind wants something to grab onto while practicing mindful breathing; I get it. Let it grab onto your breath.

Moving slowly, release your hands. During all our JustBE mindfulness practices, we slow down our usual pace. Moving more slowly than usual can feel uncomfortable, but in time we will become more comfortable with this. And you'll get to feel, see and hear more of what's going on both outside and inside of you.

(This next part requires you to be on a chair.) Grab your left elbow with your right hand and grab your right elbow with your left hand. Bend forward between your knees and hang your head down like a rag doll for five mindful breaths. Allow your spine to lengthen with each exhale. Then slowly come up, lift your gaze and take a full deep breath, exhaling out with the softest, kindest "shhhhhhhh" sound. Repeat "shhhhhhhh" twice when you exhale. Let it soften your entire body.

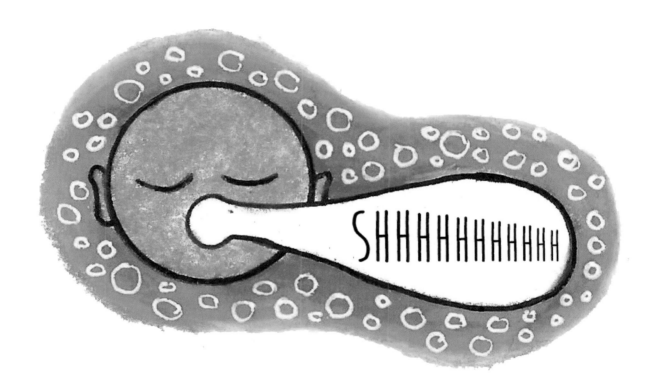

Handjam

To prepare for the handjam, bring your elbows to your sides (your waist) and let your palms come open. Take a deep inhalation, exhale fully and begin repeating the phrase TRULY LISTEN (five times aloud, five times silently) while tapping your fingers. When you are finished, place your left hand over your heart and your right hand over your left. Stay here for 10 mindful breaths. Let's mindfully breathe together.

Wisdom

When we listen carefully, we notice so much is said besides just words. What does this mean to you? When you truly listen and stay present, you'll notice the speaker's expressions and gestures as well as your own. This is a language of its own! You'll also become aware of when you get distracted. This is completely normal—we all get distracted. Simply notice the feeling and come back to the conversation.

Mindfulness in Action

Sometimes when we listen, we're only thinking about how we're going to respond. Notice when this happens and come back to the conversation with awareness. You offer the speaker a huge dose of kindness with your willingness to stay present. To truly listen is a practice, so it *takes* practice.

Honor

Take a deep mindful breath. With hands placed over our heart (left hand over heart and right hand on top of the left), honor yourself by nodding your chin down ever so slightly to your own wise heart and mind. Honor those around you in the same way. Have a mindful day!

WHAT DO YOU LOOK AND FEEL LIKE WHEN YOU ARE LISTENED TO? DRAW A PICTURE AND/OR DESCRIBE IT IN WORDS.

4) Share and Listen

Come into your mindfulness posture. Breathe mindfully and settle into the posture.

Today's handjam is SHARE AND LISTEN.

Mindfulness

Picture yourself sitting and watching a beautiful sunset. Imagine that you are surrounded by your favorite people and, one by one, each person shares a story from his or her day. The next time someone talks to you, bring your full attention to the conversation. Soften your eyes, relax the muscles in your face and neck and breathe calmly as you listen generously. Notice what happens between you and the person you are listening to. Now, sit on a chair and interlace your hands behind your lower back. Inhale, lifting your chin up while pulling your shoulders down and making your arms super-straight. As you pull your arms long, the front of your chest will open wide. Then exhale, rolling your torso forward and down, head hanging toward the ground, while pulling your hands away from your body. Make your arms as straight as possible to help open up the area around your heart. Roll up slowly. Repeat twice.

INTERLACE HANDS BEHIND LOWER BACK

Handjam

Now let's prepare for our handjam. Bring your elbows to your sides. Breathe in mindfully. Exhale fully. Repeat the phrase SHARE AND LISTEN (five times aloud, five times silently) while you tap your fingers. Then place your left hand over your heart and your right hand over your left. Stay here for 10 mindful breaths. Let's mindfully breathe together.

Wisdom

When we mindfully listen, we are connecting to both ourselves and the person we are listening to. Notice the impulse to want to interrupt and respond while the other person is talking. This is a normal impulse, yet we can learn to tame it by practicing to take a pause when this happens and just listen. Listening is an art form. Just like a painting takes time to create and fine-tune, our skills for listening require the same kind of patience and presence.

Mindfulness in Action

Sharing our true feelings—the fun stuff and the hard stuff—with the people we care for and who care for us is what makes life meaningful. Mindfulness practices like this one can help us with both sharing and listening. If it feels right, today try sharing a meaningful memory with others you trust will listen. Notice what happens as you share and they listen. Notice what you feel in response.

Honor

Place your hands over your heart, and take a deep mindful breath and honor your ability to share and listen. Nod your head down a bit to acknowledge the wisdom of your heart and mind. Honor the ability of others to share and listen as well. Have a mindful day!

5) Finger Labyrinth for Peace Within

Today's handjam is I AM PEACE.

Mindfulness

A labyrinth, with its twists and turns, is similar to a maze. Nature often reveals labyrinth, spiral-like patterns, sometimes in beautiful seashells, the way a creek wraps around rocks and trees, or how our earth orbits the sun each day. We can see swirling labyrinth patterns in a rose and in a wave, as it forms and rolls onto the shore. Labyrinths have been found in ancient cultures throughout the world, stretching from Greece to Peru, Ireland and Egypt. It's interesting that all of these different civilizations used a shared technique—the labyrinth—to connect more deeply to the earth and to themselves. Centuries ago, labyrinths might be drawn in the sand or laid out with rocks or tiles. People would walk these maze-like paths as a way to slow down, breathe and JustBE. Some ancient labyrinths extend to almost a hundred feet! Keeping all of this in mind, I've provided a finger labyrinth for you. It has the same effects as walking a labyrinth: Both require us to deliberately slow down while we try to stay within the lines and to pause at the center point for a moment of stillness. The busy world around you falls away, giving you a chance to go inward and JustBE. At the center point of the labyrinth, we add a positive intention. From there, we trace our way back to where we began, bringing our experience full circle.

To begin, place your finger labyrinth in front of you on a flat surface. Place your pointer finger at the beginning of the labyrinth where it says "start here." Pause here for three breaths. Do what you normally do at the beginning of each mindfulness practice, bringing awareness to your body, your breathing and your mind. Now, SLOWLY move your finger through the labyrinth until you reach the center. Pause here for three breaths while you breathe in "I AM PEACE" to your mind, body and heart. Trace your finger back to the entrance of the labyrinth where you began.

Notice what you felt like before and after moving through the labyrinth. Notice if anything changed.

START HERE

Handjam

Bring your elbows to your sides and let your palms fall open. Take a mindful breath in, and exhale with awareness. Now begin repeating the phrase I AM PEACE (five times aloud, five times silently) while you tap your fingers. Place your left hand over your heart and your right hand over your left. Stay here for 10 mindful breaths. Let's mindfully breathe together.

Wisdom

This is a good reminder that peace begins and ends with you. This means you get to choose how you want to respond to whatever arises around you. The finger labyrinth beautifully illustrates how you can flow through twists and turns with ease, mindfully moving through the beginning, middle and end of an experience.

Mindfulness in Action

A few times throughout the day, take a moment to notice the beginning, middle and end of each breath. Notice how each moment and each breath is new. Remain curious and see how bringing more awareness to each moment might change the outcome of your experience.

Honor

Take a deep mindful breath and honor yourself by nodding your chin down ever so slightly to your own wise heart and mind. Honor those around you in the same way. Have a mindful day!

On page 99, there is a black-and-white finger labyrinth for you to print out.

WHAT DOES NOTICING THE BEGINNING, MIDDLE OR END OF AN EXPERIENCE FEEL LIKE INSIDE YOUR MIND AND BODY? DRAW A PICTURE OR DESCRIBE IT IN WORDS.

6) I Have Support

Let's begin by getting into our mindfulness posture. Take your time and settle into a comfortable, alert sitting posture.

The handjam for today is I HAVE SUPPORT.

Mindfulness

We all start out as babies, completely vulnerable and dependent on others in our world. As we grow, we become more independent, and yet all of us still feel vulnerable at times, especially when we're learning something new. Learning how to JustBE may take some time to become comfortable with, because it is asking you to slow down, pause and observe what is happening in each moment. Some days you will feel at ease in your JustBE practice; other days, you won't. This isn't good or bad. It's part of learning how to be okay with however you are feeling and finding comfort right where you are. It takes practice and self-compassion or kindness toward yourself. You're strengthening your ability to JustBE right now!!!

In honor of our sixth practice, I will share a dear memory of a special kind of support I received when I was six years old. I used to spend a lot of time wandering around tennis clubs at that age while my siblings took part in competitions. I remember befriending an older woman, who spoke Spanish and not a word of English, at a tennis club I often went to. We would wander aimlessly around the club, looking at nature. I spoke no Spanish but loved being around her. I didn't know the words back then to describe this experience, but how I felt in her presence has stayed with me all these years. She made me feel happy, comfortable and perfectly at ease. Her kindness transcended words.

Place your hands on your knees, and move your ribcage in a big circle five times in one direction. Try to keep the rest of your body still. Now move your ribcage in a circle five times in the other direction. Have fun with it. Notice how your lower body supports your upper body while moving in this way.

Handjam

To prepare for the handjam, bring your elbows to your sides (your waist), and let your palms come open. Inhale deeply, exhale fully and repeat the phrase, I HAVE SUPPORT (five times aloud, five times silently) while you tap your fingers. Place your left hand over your heart and your right hand over your left. Stay here for 10 mindful breaths. Let's mindfully breathe together.

Wisdom

When we focus on where we find support, we can bring this into our awareness in times of need. This is how we begin to strengthen the peace within us. Pause and bring into your mind someone who has offered you support, or someone from whom you'd like support. Pause and close or half-close your eyes. Bring your attention to the way your breath feels coming in and going out. What would that supportive person say to soothe you? Pause again and breathe in this question. What would his or her face look like? Pause again. Imagine that person's kindness surrounding your whole being.

Mindfulness in Action

We're going to do a fun practice on the next page (practice #7) called "Hands Are Extensions of Our Hearts" to help us clearly see where we find support. Once you're finished, don't forget to do the Honor part of our JustBE practice.

Honor

Take a deep mindful breath and honor yourself by nodding your chin down ever so slightly to your own wise heart and mind. Honor those around you in the same way. Have a mindful day!

7) Hands Are Extensions of Our Hearts

Let's take a moment to express where we have support.

We don't often give much thought to our hands, but if you think about it, our hands do an endless number of things for us each day. In a way, our hands are extensions of our hearts. Let's take a peek into what flows out of your heart and into your hands.

Instructions: On the opposite page is one example of what we are about to do. Grab a blank sheet of paper and colored pencils or markers. Place the palm of one hand (the one you don't write with) flat on the paper with fingers spread wide. Now, starting at your wrist, trace your hand. Keep the pencil or marker close to your skin. When you're finished, take a moment to think about two people in your life who are important to you. Draw or write who these people are within the outlines of your pinky and ring fingers. In the spaces of your middle and pointer fingers, draw or write the names of two places you hold dear—places that make you feel at ease and happy. Then draw and/or write one thing you treasure in the space of your thumb area. Your words and images don't need to fit inside the drawing of your hand. You can use all the white space on the paper freely. When you're done, take a look at all that you hold close to your heart on your hand. When you find yourself in need of support, bring this image to mind and let it lift you up.

ZOE

MAYA

RED ROCKS COLORADO

MEDITATION CUSHION

MY DOG BARDO

8) Kindness Matters

Let's begin our JustBE practice by coming into our mindfulness posture. Breathe mindfully and find the stillness that lives within. Try imagining a lake that is completely calm. The top of the lake is smooth and still. By bringing attention to your breath, you can find this same kind of stillness, because it allows your focus to move from your thoughts into JustBE-ing. Your JustBE practice will help you dive in and find moments of stillness. These moments of stillness are like vitamins, nourishing you and giving you access to your wise mind that knows how to pause and respond mindfully. It's a practice, so let's practice. Be gentle with yourself.

Today's handjam is KINDNESS MATTERS.

Mindfulness

Commit to not adding more aggression to the world. Tolerance and kindness are needed, and you can start creating it within yourself, right now, by practicing how to JustBE. Creating more tolerance will directly enhance your relationships. If you think about it, the only difference between you and people who flip their lid is simply a choice. You get to thoughtfully choose what you want to say and do. The more you pause and act from a calm, peaceful place, the more ownership you take of your life.

A friend of mine who was in medical school treated a patient who was suffering from liver failure. During her stay in the hospital, they connected in a special way. Eventually, the patient got better, left the hospital and went on her way. Twenty years later, out of the blue, she sent my friend a photo of the two of them together, along with a message expressing how much my friend had helped her. That patient is now an intensive care nurse, healthy and living a full life. I tell this story because you never really know how your words and actions will affect others. But what you can know for sure is that they matter—and that our kindness matters, too.

Handjam

To prepare for the handjam, bring your elbows to your sides (your waist), and let your palms come open. Take a deep inhalation, exhale fully and begin repeating the phrase KINDNESS MATTERS (five times aloud, five times silently) while tapping your fingers. Place your left hand over your heart and your right hand over your left. Stay here for 10 mindful breaths. Let's mindfully breathe together.

Wisdom

I am continually amazed at how a desired outcome can occur by merely waiting rather than immediately reacting. I am in no way suggesting that you be passive or to not respond or act when needed, but rather to wait until feelings of confusion, anger and/or disappointment pass. Pause until you can see clearly and respond from that place; wait until the feeling that grabbed you no longer grabs you. That said, it's also essential to attend to the discomfort you feel while waiting. Breathe into it, go for a walk, rest or shake your hands out vigorously to release the energy.

Mindfulness in Action

Now we are going to learn and practice something simple and powerful. We are going to shake! YES, shake. But first let me explain why. In one of my graduate school classes, we watched a video about a bear and her cubs being threatened by a mountain lion. The mama bear successfully warded off the predator and took her cubs to safety. Then she moved a few steps away and began shaking. Her whole body shook for a short time. Then she stepped back to her cubs and they went on their way. The wisdom from the mama bear is this: When a threat appears, we must allow the energy of that situation to move through us completely so that we can feel better.

Ok, you ready? Start shaking your hands super-fast. Now your feet. Now your shoulders forward, back, up and down. Shake your head all around. Now shake your head, feet, shoulders and your whole body super-fast all at once for at least one full minute. Let go of any thoughts about looking silly. When you're done, place your feet flat on the ground, and take three mindful breaths. Notice how you feel after you shake.

While doing this practice, you're practicing self-compassion—kindness plus action. This week, try to shake whenever you're feeling impatient or frustrated, or to settle a busy mind. Find someone who will shake with you as well and have a little fun with it.

Honor

After all that shaking, let's settle in. Take a deep mindful breath and honor (always with hands over the heart) yourself by nodding your chin down ever so slightly to your own wise heart and mind. Honor those around you in the same way. Have a mindful day!

HOW DID SHAKING HELP CALM YOUR MIND AND BODY? DRAW A PICTURE OR DESCRIBE IT IN WORDS.

9) Strong Heart, Strong Mind

Let's take our time and come into our mindfulness posture. Allow your body to settle in and breathe mindfully.

The handjam for today is STRONG HEART, STRONG MIND.

Mindfulness

When my family moved back to Miami a few years ago, we didn't know anyone in our neighborhood or school. It felt lonely at times, so we turned to nature while we adjusted to our new city. We would go to the bridge nearby and watch how pelicans dove for fish every evening as the sun set. Pelicans have incredible eyesight and can spot a fish clearly while flying far above the water. Whenever they detected a fish, they'd dive straight down into the water, super-fast like a torpedo. Then they would pop right back up to the surface, sometimes with fish in their mouths. Fun Fact: Did you know pelicans can't sink? It's true! Pelicans have a special sauce within their feathers that makes them rise to the surface after they dive.

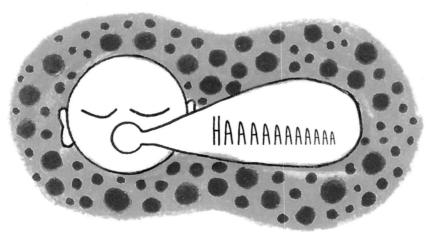

We can use this example of the pelicans to remind us that we, too, can rise to the surface when things feel challenging. For my family, pelicans were a reminder that we could try new things with courage and precision. This helped us dive into new situations, knowing that no matter what, we'd eventually bob back up.

Inhale through your nose and lift your shoulders toward your ears. Think about how, when there's discomfort around you, you can stay rooted in your own inner strength. Exhale, and drop your shoulders down while making a loud sound of haaaaaaaaaaaa through your mouth. Repeat four times.

Handjam

Let's prepare for our handjam. Bring your elbows to your sides (your waist) and let your palms come open Inhale deeply, exhale fully and begin repeating the phrase STRONG HEART, STRONG MIND (five times aloud, five times silently) while you tap your fingers. Bring your left hand to your heart and your right hand over your left. Stay here for 10 mindful breaths. Let's mindfully breathe together.

Wisdom

Being strong in your heart and mind means being aware of and understanding how you feel. Take a moment to pause and feel into the thoughts traveling through your mind. What's the first thing you notice? Bring your attention to your hands on your heart. Do you feel calm, distracted, joyful or something else? Check the feeling faces chart on page 14, if you need guidance. Knowing what you feel and naming those feelings will help you understand yourself better. The cool thing is that by understanding yourself, you understand others better, too!

Mindfulness in Action

Notice today how your thoughts affect how your body feels, and how sensations in your body affect your mind. For example, you may aspire to "tighten up your habits," at home or school, and, as a result, your body might tighten up as well. The key here is to notice the connection between your bodily sensations—tightness, pulling, warmth, chilliness, throbbing, jitters, relaxation, etc. Once you notice the connection, you can act on it. How? By bringing awareness to what you're thinking and feeling, and softening into it. We have learned how to do this at the start of each JustBE practice as we come into the mindfulness posture. Focus on the breath, while elongating the exhale. That kind of mindful breathing, and softening into what's happening now, represents a sort of kindness that you offer yourself, and it strengthens your heart/mind connection.

Honor

Take a deep mindful breath and honor yourself by nodding your chin down ever so slightly to your own wise heart and mind. Honor those around you in the same way. Have a mindful day!

10) Pausing Is Wise

Let's begin by getting into our mindfulness posture. Pause and take a deep mindful breath. Your breath is the bridge that connects your mind to your body. Over time, your mind and body will know exactly what to do whenever you hear the words, "Let's begin by getting into our mindfulness posture." It's an invitation to link your mind and body through your breath.

The handjam for today is PAUSING IS WISE.

Mindfulness

Have you ever tried to guess what other people are thinking? It's tempting, but assumptions we make often turn out to be false. That's why making assumptions usually works against us. Imagine that you notice someone looking at you. Instead of assuming that that person doesn't like your shoes or is mad at you, tell yourself this: "I'm not sure what that look might mean, but I'm just going to take a few deep breaths and not assume that I know the answers." It might not feel satisfying, but sometimes practicing resting in a place of "not knowing" strengthens our ability to be okay in that moment.

Inhale deeply. As you exhale, interlace your hands behind your head at the base of your neck, squeezing your shoulder blades together so that your elbows extend back opening your heart center. Begin to twist right to left really fast. Keep going to the count of 30. Go! When you are done, lift both arms out straight to both sides and bring them over your head, touching your palms together. Stretch your arms high. Ground your feet into the floor while also reaching up high with your arms. Breathe in deeply. Exhale and bring your palms together at your heart center. Take three mindful breaths.

Handjam

To prepare for the handjam, bring your elbows to your sides (your waist) and let your palms come open. Inhale deeply, exhale fully and begin repeating the phrase PAUSING IS WISE (five times aloud, five times silently) while tapping your fingers. Place your left hand over your heart and your right hand over your left. Stay here for 10 mindful breaths. Let's mindfully breathe together.

Wisdom

How does pausing help? When is a good time to pause? How can you remember to pause? One way is to remember the consequences of reacting when you're angry or frustrated without pausing first. This is a good step to remembering the benefits of pausing. When you notice that activated feeling bubbling up inside you, take it as a signal that you need to pause, step away if necessary and breathe for a moment—or many moments. Acting and speaking from a calmer, clearer place gives you a better chance of getting a positive result. Pausing is kind—and kind of magical.

Mindfulness in Action

Instead of immediately reacting to things today, find the power in the pause. Your awareness is being strengthened by practicing being present to what arises that will enable you to take a few seconds before you respond to a situation so that you can respond with your wise mind. Bring to your mind's eye the image of the completely still lake that we talked about in an earlier practice. The bottom of the lake is completely calm, undisturbed by the environment above the surface. Your wise mind is able to remain calm, despite what chaos may be going on around you. By accessing your wise mind (the part of your mind that is just like the calm waters at the bottom of the lake), you'll find the clarity you need to choose mindful words and actions. It's a powerful and extraordinary skill. Not buying into this? Try it out and see what happens. You got this!

Honor

Take a deep mindful breath and honor yourself by nodding your chin down ever so slightly to your own wise heart and mind. Honor those around you in the same way. Even honor your dog/cat or other family pet. My dog loves sitting next to me while I practice on my cushion, so I often honor her! Have a mindful day!

HOW DO YOU LOOK AND FEEL WHEN YOU REMEMBER TO PAUSE? DRAW A PICTURE OR DESCRIBE IT IN WORDS.

11) My Words Have Power

Take your time while coming into your mindfulness posture. Begin to mindfully breathe. Notice if your body is tight, and soften into that area by using your mindful breathing.

The handjam for today is MY WORDS HAVE POWER.

Mindfulness

Let's think about sounds. Sounds can be soothing, upsetting, sad, happy or exciting. Take a few seconds to listen to the sounds that come from within you. What do you hear? The sound of your breath? Your stomach rumbling? Now, picture someone you know who has a soothing, calming voice. Bring that person to mind for a moment and think of how his or her voice makes you feel. It doesn't need to be someone you know. It could be a singer or someone on TV whom you like and admire.

Now, snap your fingers 20 times. If it's hard to snap, rub your palms together really fast. Listen to the music it creates. Is it loud, calming, annoying or fun?

Imagine how your tone of voice affects others and why it's important to be mindful (aware) of the words you use and how you sound. When your tone and your words are thoughtfully composed, it's like two puzzle pieces coming together. Everything matches up and clicks right into place.

Handjam

To prepare for the handjam, bring your elbows to your sides (your waist), and let your palms come open. Take a deep inhalation, exhale fully and begin repeating the phrase MY WORDS HAVE POWER (five times aloud, five times silently) while tapping your fingers. Place your left hand over your heart and your right hand over your left. Stay here for 10 mindful breaths. Let's mindfully breathe together.

Wisdom

How do our words have power? Think of someone who's spoken the kindest words to you and the feeling that came along with that. Think of how you can spread more of that feeling into this world. Your words leave unseen footprints on this earth. Just like oak trees are here to provide shade and produce acorns, you also are meant to leave gifts on this earth.

YOU'RE MEANT TO LEAVE GIFTS ON THE EARTH

Mindfulness in Action

Practice speaking a little more slowly than you usually do. This may feel slightly weird, but try it anyway! Sometimes our minds can feel like they are moving fast with lots of thoughts, and we may speak quickly as a result. By slowing down, you can start to feel the power of your words AND how they affect those around you. For instance, the phrase "I should" has subtle negative connotations. So rather than saying something like, "I should be better at math," say, "I want to be better at math because I know I'm capable of learning new things." Notice the difference in the way those two statements sound and make you feel when you say them. Today, practice replacing the "shoulds," with "I want to _____ because _____." See how this simple switch in words makes a positive impact on your mood.

Honor

Take a deep mindful breath and honor yourself by nodding your chin down ever so slightly to your own wise heart and mind. Honor those around you in the same way. If it feels comfortable, look into the eyes of those around you. You can offer kindness through your eyes. Have a mindful day!

HOW HAS SLOWING DOWN WHILE YOU SPEAK AND BEING MORE AWARE OF YOUR WORDS HELPED YOU? DRAW A PICTURE OR DESCRIBE IT IN WORDS.

12) I Am Okay

Let's begin by getting into our mindfulness posture. Bring your attention to your hands, which are folded into a peace ball. (It's kind of cool to have an imaginary ball of peace in your lap.) Soften your arms and shoulders and imagine your peace ball in a color you love. Imagine it swirling around in your hands. Remember, your hands are extensions of your heart.

The handjam for today is I AM OKAY. Go to www.mindfulnikki.com/videos to see this handjam (and many others) being done by kids in an elementary school in Miami.

Mindfulness

The idea of talking to yourself might sound silly, but telling yourself, "I am okay," is actually quite empowering. It's something you can tell yourself whenever you don't feel okay and want to calm your body and mind in the present moment. Practice repeating this simple phrase to yourself when you're having a hard moment: "I'm okay even though the things around me don't feel okay." Sometimes you need to repeat a phrase until you believe it. Let's do it together. Check your mindfulness posture with your back as straight as it can be comfortably. Breathe mindfully and extend your exhale longer than your inhale. Close or half-close your eyes. Take a moment to imagine your feet sending roots down into the core of the earth, and that these roots support and hold you. What does that feel like? Pause and feel into that. Now, repeat aloud, "I'm okay even though the things around me might not feel okay." Maybe write this down somewhere where you can see it often as a reminder. Say it to yourself regularly, and you'll begin to feel as strong as a tree that's deeply rooted in the earth. No matter what storms come, you may bend and sway, but your roots stay strong and intact, just like you. Bring both hands in front of your heart and place your right hand on top of your left, palms facing your body. Interlace your thumbs making a "butterfly" position with your hands and start *alternately* tapping your hands on your chest. (Refer to the illustration and/or go to www.mindfulnikki.com/videos to see how it's done.)

The tips of your fingers should be just under your collarbone area. Do this for at least 30 taps.

Butterfly tapping can be a quick way to find your way back to calm. Practice it on your own when you need to find some calm. Observe how you feel afterward. Anything different? If so, what?

Handjam

To prepare for the handjam, bring your elbows to your sides (your waist), and let your palms come open. Take a deep inhalation, exhale fully and begin repeating the phrase I AM OKAY (five times aloud, five times silently) while you tap your fingers. Place your left hand over your heart and your right hand over your left. Stay here for 10 mindful breaths. Let's mindfully breathe together.

Wisdom

The handjam empowers us. It's a reminder that there is ALWAYS peace inside of us, independent of what is going on around us. This is great news: Once you know in your wise heart, mind and body that you can find ways to be okay, then you can also realize that peace begins with you. And once you know it, you can't un-know it. It's your golden ticket to JustBE!

Now, feel into your heart center where your hands are, and connect inward.

Let's sit in silence for three breaths while we keep our intention in mind: "I AM OKAY."

Mindfulness in Action

The fun part of Mindfulness in Action is noticing when you can use your mindfulness superpower skills in your everyday experiences. The first step is observing how you feel. (Refer to feeling faces chart on page 14.) The second step is choosing an action (such as the handjam, "I AM OKAY") that will help you feel more balanced. Find moments to practice.

Honor

Place your hands over your heart. Take a deep mindful breath and honor yourself by nodding your chin down ever so slightly to your own wise heart and mind. Honor those around you in the same way. Have a mindful day!

HOW DO YOU LOOK AND FEEL WHEN YOU PRACTICE THE "I AM OKAY" HAND JAM? WHAT CHANGES? DRAW A PICTURE OR DESCRIBE IT IN WORDS.

13) Change Is Okay

Let's come into our mindfulness posture.

The handjam for today is CHANGE IS OKAY.

Mindfulness

Settle into where you are right now by bringing your attention to your breath. Place your hands in a peace ball in your lap. Close or half-close your eyes. Find stillness by counting each breath. Take three mindful breaths. Count silently, and after you reach 3, notice what you are feeling. Take a look at the feeling faces chart on page 14. Match what you are feeling with one of the faces. Don't worry about getting it right or wrong, because you can't. Just choose the first picture that feels connected to what you are feeling now. What are the thoughts related to how you feel?

It might help to take a peek at the list of feelings when your needs are being met or not met on pages 11-13. Breathe mindfully again to the count of 3. Close or half-close your eyes. When you are finished, ask yourself what do you notice while in stillness? Is your mind super-busy? Are you restless? How long does it take to settle into stillness? Our feelings change often. This is normal. Knowing what we feel and how to name what we feel will better help us get what we need! This is called being emotionally intelligent (EQ), and the good news is we all can learn how to become more aware of our feelings. You just did! Congrats!

Clap your hands together super-fast for 30 seconds, and then slowly for 30 seconds. Now clap at a regular pace. You deserve a round of applause.

Handjam

To prepare for the handjam, bring your elbows to your sides (your waist), and let your palms come open. Take a deep inhalation, exhale fully and begin repeating the phrase CHANGE IS OKAY (five times aloud, five times silently) while tapping your fingers. Place your left hand over your heart and your right hand over your left. Stay here for 10 mindful breaths. Let's mindfully breathe together.

Wisdom

Things are ever-changing, like our body changes as we grow older, and even the weather changes from moment to moment. Sometimes big changes occur, like moving to a new city or school, and we need to find a way to be okay. At times, your mind might go to a future event that hasn't happened yet, leaving you feeling unsettled and restless. Or your mind may go to a past event, going over it and trying to make sense of it. The good news is that we can find ease within changes by practicing our mindful breathing and training ourselves to come into the present moment. It is then you start to feel okay with whatever arises.

Mindfulness in Action

There is a short pause between each "in-breath" and "out-breath," between riding to school and walking into school and between the time we wake up and the time we get out of bed. Noticing these in-between moments helps you slow down and feel into your heart, mind and body, giving you a greater understanding of what you are feeling and why. Today, every time before you walk outside, get on your bike or walk toward the subway, practice PAUSING to mindfully breathe three times before heading on your way. See what happens as you slow down. Maybe you'll notice those precious moments of transition are agitating. Maybe you'll notice that your breathing is shallow. Maybe you'll notice that these three breaths bring you a bit of peace and calm. Just notice. Observe the sensations that arise in your body and the thoughts that come into your mind. After doing this practice myself for eight weeks, I was amazed to find that those three breaths often felt like an eternity. It made me aware of how rushed I was and helped me slow down. By mindfully slowing down, you can start to feel okay with big and little changes in life.

Honor

Take a deep mindful breath and honor yourself by nodding your chin down ever so slightly to your own wise heart and mind. Honor those around you in the same way. Have a mindful day!

14) I Choose Peace

We're at the point where your body just naturally knows what to do when we begin the JustBE practice. *Hint*: mindfulness posture, peace ball, mindful breathing, mindful movements.

Our handjam for today is I CHOOSE PEACE.

NO

YES

Mindfulness

Sometimes we firmly believe that we are right about something, and we want to tell other people that they're wrong. The catch? When we get stuck on the need to be right, it can cause disagreements. What does the thought "I'm right and you're wrong" feel like inside your mind, and in your body? Maybe your chest gets tight, or you clench your teeth. Notice that feeling. Listen to your breath. Moving slowly, drop your chin toward your chest and then lift it up to the sky. You're saying yes with your head. Now shake your head from side to side, as if to say no. It's important to feel good and clear about both our *yeses* and our *noes*.

Handjam

To prepare for the handjam, bring your elbows to your sides (your waist), and let your palms come open. Take a deep inhalation, exhale fully and begin repeating the phrase I CHOOSE PEACE (five times aloud, five times silently) while you tap your fingers. Place your left hand over your heart and your right hand over your left. Stay here for 10 mindful breaths. Let's mindfully breathe together.

Wisdom

It's been my experience that when I loosen the need to be right, even when I disagree greatly with the other person's view, the exchange between us softens. There is a way to hold and state your views, without having to be right, and prove the other wrong. By choosing peace and kindness over the need to be right, you offer more peace and kindness to the world. Thank you: The world needs more of what you have to offer!

Mindfulness in Action

Consider this saying: "When you want to be right, choose peace instead." The next time you're in a discussion and are struck by the need to be right, take a deep breath, pause and listen with an open mind to the other person. Observe what happens within you when you act in this way. Then respond with kindness instead of having to prove that you're right. This might sound like, "That's an interesting point of view—I'm going to think about it for a bit." Or you might choose to remain silent and see what it feels like to listen. Whether you choose to respond with or without words doesn't matter; there's no right or wrong. Observe what happens between you and the other person when your mindfulness informs your decision.

Honor

Place your hands back over your heart. Take a deep mindful breath and honor yourself by nodding your chin down ever so slightly to your own wise heart and mind. Honor those around you in the same way. Honor the peace you are offering to the world as well. Have a mindful day!

WHAT DO YOU LOOK AND FEEL LIKE WHEN YOU PAUSE AND RELEASE THE NEED TO BE RIGHT? HOW DOES IT HELP A SITUATION? WHAT CHANGES? DRAW A PICTURE OR DESCRIBE IT IN WORDS.

15) Flexible Spine, Flexible Mind

Settle into your mindfulness posture. Notice your shoulders. Soften them back and down; see how this affects your breathing. Lift your spine/back as straight as possible. Stay here for three breaths and just observe. Let's breathe together.

Today's handjam is FLEXIBLE SPINE, FLEXIBLE MIND.

Mindfulness

Do you ever purposely stop to consider your feelings? Feelings help us understand both ourselves and the world around us. Finding the right words to express our feelings to the people around us is so important. It's also essential to know the people we can reach in times of need or when we feel uncomfortable. Think about a time when you felt safe and comfortable telling someone how you feel. What did that person do or say that left you feeling good about the situation? Take this moment to check in with your own feelings. Are you confused? Content? Frustrated? Anxious? Happy? (Refer to the feelings and feeling faces charts on page 11-14.)

Now, let's do more of those awesome spine roll stretches that we always do at the start of our JustBE practice. Place your hands on your knees. Breathe in and send your chest out, shoulders back and lift your chin to the sky by letting your head drop back. Really extend your chin up as high as possible. Your chest should be wide open in this position, allowing you to take in more breath. Then, as you exhale, round your back and bring your chin toward your chest head tilting downward. Your arms will become straight and you should be able to feel a nice stretch in the back of your neck, shoulders and in your spine as well. Repeat four times moving as slow as possible. Flow through these movements by synchronizing your breath to the movements.

Handjam

To prepare for the handjam, bring your elbows to your sides (your waist), and let your palms come open. Take a deep inhalation, exhale fully and begin repeating the phrase FLEXIBLE SPINE, FLEXIBLE MIND (five times aloud, five times silently) while you tap fingers. Place your left hand over your heart and your right hand over your left. Stay here for 10 mindful breaths. Let's mindfully breathe together.

Wisdom

A flexible spine equals a flexible mind. Interesting idea, right? This suggests your mind affects your body and vice versa. Imagine in your mind's eye a visual of a telephone pole and a palm tree. How strong and rigid they both are, and need to be, to withstand rough weather. Similarly, we are sometimes rigid like a telephone pole, unbending and inflexible because we think we need to be that way in order to withstand a tough situation. But if you watch a telephone pole and a palm tree in a hurricane, you will see that palm trees are able to bend nearly in half without breaking, while telephone poles, being so stiff, simply snap when the winds become too strong. I live in Miami, so I've been through a few hurricanes and have seen this firsthand! The wisdom here is this: When your body feels super-tight like a telephone pole, use your JustBE skills to return to your natural bendy and flexible way of being so that you can weather storms with more ease.

Mindfulness in Action

Today, notice your mind and body's ability to adapt and become flexible to what arises. Or notice the opposite, when you tense up. When your belly rumbles, letting you know you need food, it's the language your body uses to get your attention. For example, you might have arranged to hang out with a friend after school, but at the last second, plans changed. It's normal to feel disappointed. You may notice that you clench your jaw, or that your neck tightens in response. Your body is a wise teacher—listen to what it's trying to tell you.

Honor

Take a deep mindful breath and honor yourself by nodding your chin down ever so slightly to your own wise heart and mind. Honor those around you in the same way. Have a mindful day!

16) Interconnected

Come into your mindfulness posture. Begin your mindful breathing and connect your awareness to your breath. Feel how your breath moves through you.

The handjam for today is INTERCONNECTED.

Mindfulness

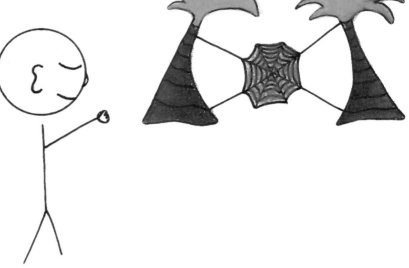

One day I saw a spider web that stretched between my house and a palm tree. A tropical storm came through and when I ventured outside the next day, I saw that against all odds, the spider web had weathered the storm! How could something be so fragile yet so strong?

Think about how a spider anchors its web: It attaches the web to something trusty and solid.

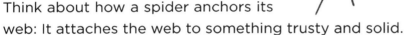

Now you are going to see how bendy your body is by taking your right foot and laying it on top of your left thigh. Allow the heel of your right foot to come up as high as it comfortably can towards where your leg and torso meet. Let your right knee relax down as much as you can. Now take your left foot and encourage it gently to lift up and over your right leg and rest your left foot on top of your right thigh. This is the lotus posture. Oooouch! Your left leg may not be able to come on top of your right leg just yet. That is okay. But play around with it a bit, and with time and practice, your body will bend more and more.

A spider's web may be kind of gross to you—I must admit I definitely don't like getting caught in one. But you can't deny the way this tiny being creates an intricate net that connects and interconnects in ways even the most gifted of physicists couldn't have come up with. And that it is both strong and fragile all at once. Wow! A spider web can remind us of how we are connected to the rest of the world, and how to be strong and fragile all at once.

Handjam

To prepare for the handjam, bring your elbows to your sides (your waist), and let your palms come open. Take a deep inhalation, exhale fully and begin repeating the phrase INTERCONNECTED (five times aloud, five times silently) while tapping your fingers. Place your left hand over your heart and your right hand over your left. Stay here for 10 mindful breaths. Let's mindfully breathe together.

Wisdom

Take a moment to feel into your hands over your heart. Breathe these words in: When we feel interconnected, we feel an intimate relationship, and trust with the earth. This translates to feeling trust within ourselves. When we feel interconnected, we cannot feel alone.

Mindfulness in Action

When you can, connect with nature and notice how the sun shines on the plants, how the rain feeds the plants and how the butterflies and animals depend on the sun, rain and plants for food and shelter. Notice how you relate to the natural world around you by taking moments to observe the simple beauties of nature. Where I sit in this moment, there is a passion flower vine outside the window. The flowers are blooming, lots of butterflies are circling around and big red ants are confidently walking the vines, as if walking on a tightrope with no net to catch them if they fall. Taking a few minutes to watch these tiny creatures pass by gives my mind a break from figuring things out, and I can rest in the simplicity and wonders of nature. Take a few minutes today to do the same.

Honor

Take a deep mindful breath and honor yourself by nodding your chin down ever so slightly to your own wise heart and mind. Notice how placing your hands over your heart connects you to a strong, beautiful and interconnected place. Honor the people around you. Have a mindful day!

17) I Believe in Me

Come into your mindfulness posture. Bring your awareness to your posture. Make small adjustments until you settle in.

The handjam for today is I BELIEVE IN ME.

Mindfulness

Do you feel good about yourself when you study for a test and do well? What if no one pats you on the back to say, "Well done?" Do you still feel good about your efforts? It's important to recognize your hard work and successes, even if other people don't applaud you for them. Take a moment to think of something you'd like to congratulate yourself on that you did well. Find what motivates you from the inside, and give yourself the pat on the back that you deserve! Take one hand and pat yourself on your shoulder and say to yourself, "Well done." Repeat that action on the other side. Repeat this twice. This is self-compassion (kindness + action) toward yourself. We are taught to be kind to others, which is great, but we also must practice turning that kindness inward.

Handjam

To prepare for the handjam, bring your elbows to your sides (your waist), and let your palms come open. Take a deep inhalation, exhale fully and begin repeating the phrase I BELIEVE IN ME (five times aloud, five times silently) while tapping your fingers.

Place your left hand over your heart and your right hand over your left. Stay here for 10 mindful breaths. Let's mindfully breathe together.

Wisdom

We need to feel okay from within and not depend on others telling us that we are okay. Hearing compliments feels good of course, but we also want to know and believe that we can feel good about ourselves no matter what other people think about us. This takes awareness and practice.

Mindfulness in Action

Right now, bring to mind one thing, big or small, that is going well in your life. Close your eyes if it helps you focus. We often focus too much on what is not going well and what we need to work on. Turn that around today and bring what is going well front and center. Breathe into that and let your mind, body and heart believe it, too.

Honor

Take a deep mindful breath and honor yourself by nodding your chin down ever so slightly to your own wise heart and mind. Let your head hang here for three breaths. Take this moment to honor all that you are—all of it. Now, lift your head up, and engage with those around you through your eyes, taking a few extra moments to notice one another's eye color. Honor their BE-ing and have a mindful day!

18) Labyrinth of Kindness

Settle into your mindfulness posture. Find inner stillness before you begin, by extending your exhale longer than your inhale. Let's practice mindful breathing together for the next 10 breaths with our hands over our heart. Let's count silently to ourselves inside our minds.

The handjam for this practice is SPREAD COMPASSION.

Instructions: Place your finger labyrinth in front of you on a flat surface. Place your pointer finger at the beginning of your finger labyrinth where it says "start here." Pause here for three breaths before you begin. Slowly move your finger between the lines until you get to the center of the labyrinth. Pause here again for three breaths while you bring to mind someone who is having a hard time. It could be you, someone you know, or even a pet. It can be someone you know well or maybe someone you saw at school who seems to be having a hard time speaking up, learning, making friends, etc. Pick someone (or an animal) who you want to share your kindness with. After you have chosen who you want to offer kindness to, begin moving your finger through the labyrinth. As you breathe out, imagine the kindness within you creating an imaginary clear glass-like castle all around who you chose. Your kindness castle helps them feel safe, cared for and peaceful. When you come to the center of your finger labyrinth, pause here and breathe into this image for three breaths. Now, follow your finger slowly around the labyrinth back to where you began. Pause and take a mindful breath here.

START HERE

Handjam

To prepare for the handjam, bring your elbows to your sides (your waist), and let your palms come open. Take a deep inhalation, exhale fully and begin repeating the phrase SPREAD COMPASSION (five times aloud, five times silently) while tapping your fingers. Place your left hand over your heart and your right hand over your left. Stay here for three mindful breaths. Let's mindfully breathe together.

Wisdom

What did you notice while offering kindness in this way? Did anything change? Isn't it cool how we can use our imagination, breath and awareness to create positive change in ourselves and others? Pause and let this question swirl through you.

Mindfulness in Action

The finger labyrinth illustrates how you can offer a powerful non-verbal gesture of kindness to others. Today, look for opportunities to breathe kindness out onto others. This may sound silly, but there are times when offering the intention of kindness, silently, through your breath, is exactly the medicine needed. For example, I do this when I see a dog wandering the streets, or a homeless person on the grass sleeping. There are many opportunities all around us, every day, to offer up simple and beautiful acts of kindness.

Honor

Take a deep mindful breath and honor yourself by nodding your chin down ever so slightly to your own wise heart and mind. You are adding awareness to the world by practicing BE-ing aware of your thoughts, words and actions. Honor that in yourself. Honor that capability in those around you. Have a kind-ful day!

PAUSE FOR A MOMENT AND THINK OF ONE WAY YOU'D LIKE TO SPREAD COMPASSION INTO YOUR HOME, SCHOOL AND COMMUNITY. NOW, WRITE OR DRAW HOW THIS ACT OF COMPASSION WILL MAKE YOU FEEL AND HOW IT WILL MAKE THOSE RECEIVING YOUR COMPASSION FEEL.

19) Thoughts Come and Go

Let's come into our mindfulness posture.

The handjam for today is THOUGHTS COME AND GO.

Mindfulness

Imagine you are sitting on the beach, watching the ocean. Picture each wave as it rises and falls. Pause. Waves wash over the sand just like our thoughts wash over our minds, coming and going. Visualize those waves as you slowly breathe in and out. Notice the breath coming in and going out, just as waves come and go. Feel your stomach expand as you inhale and relax as you exhale. Notice, observe, no-judgments, JustBE. Be with your mindful breathing.

FLOW LIKE WATER

Close your eyes if it's comfortable, or gaze down and half-close your eyes. Observe the ebb and flow of your thoughts passing through your mind like waves coming onto shore. Notice them *without* going into trying to figure out what the thoughts mean. JustBE with whatever arises, leaving the thoughts just as they are. It takes practice JustBE-ing with the flow of what comes through your mind. The more we can relate to whatever arises with a quality of peace and calm, inevitably, the more peace and calm becomes available to us. There have been times after becoming mad or frustrated where I become hardened like an ice cube. Can you relate? There is nothing warm or soft about an ice cube! It's solid, cold and hard to break apart. But when I remember to notice and observe the thoughts that are creating this ice-cube-like response, then I have the awareness to help that feeling soften and melt, and I return once again to water and flow more easily. This is something that you have the tools to practice as well.

Handjam

To prepare for the handjam, bring your elbows to your sides (your waist), and let your palms come open. Take a deep inhalation, exhale fully and begin repeating the phrase THOUGHTS COME AND GO (five times aloud, five times silently) while tapping your fingers. Place your left hand over your heart and your right hand over your left. Stay here for 10 mindful breaths. Let's mindfully breathe together.

Wisdom

Things are changing all the time. When we can find flow within the ever-changing nature of things, we too can flow like water flows downstream—effortlessly and with grace. We are made up of mostly water, so we can flow in a similar way.

Mindfulness in Action

Nature's wisdom surrounds us, showing us the natural cycles and patterns of change. Every day, the sun rises and the sun sets. Some days, it rains or snows; the sky can be cloudy, then clear. Nature is always evolving, just like we are. Today, if a challenging moment arises, bring into your mind's eye something from nature that gives you a sense of calm. It doesn't even need to be a place you've visited. It could be an image from a video or even a picture you've seen and liked. Bring this image to mind, and imagine the colors, sounds, smells and the feeling this place enlivens in you. Your mind and body will remember this feeling, which means you can access it whenever you like.

Honor

Take a deep mindful breath and honor yourself by nodding your chin down ever so slightly to your own wise heart and mind. Honor those around you in the same way. Have a mindful day!

20) I Can JustBE

Settle into your mindfulness posture. Notice your shoulders. Soften them back and down and see how this affects your breathing. Stay here for a few seconds and just observe without judgment.

Fun Fact: Sitting up straight with your heart open, like we always do in the mindfulness posture, can positively affect your mood.

Today's handjam is I CAN JustBE.

Mindfulness

Let's think about uncertainty. There are some things we know for certain, like our routines at school. But every day, when we go to school, talk to our parents and see our friends, we don't know what they will say or do. So how do we handle not knowing what will happen next?

Begin by being kind to yourself by practicing mindful breathing. Let's practice together: Come onto a chair for this next part if you are sitting on a cushion and set your feet flat on the ground. Feel all four corners of your feet. Take a deep inhale and exhale. Now place your left hand over your heart and your right hand on top of your left. (You are used to this because this is what we do every time right after we finish doing our handjam.) Take a big breath in, and breathe out completely. Repeat four times. Feel into JustBE-ing where you are right now in this moment, and that all is well.

Handjam

To prepare for the handjam, bring your elbows to your sides (your waist), and let your palms come open. Take a deep inhalation, exhale fully and begin repeating the phrase I CAN JustBE (five times aloud, five times silently) while tapping your fingers. Place hands back over your heart, right hand over your left. Stay here for 10 mindful breaths. Let's mindfully breathe together.

Wisdom

Honoring and being kind to yourself during transitions during your day is important: It means letting your mind and body know that you can JustBE and flow. Whenever you feel uncertain about something, set your feet on the ground, close your eyes or lower your eyes down a bit and remember what it feels like to JustBE—nothing to figure out, nowhere to go, non-judgmental, present, and aware. Settling into stillness within your body will help you settle into uncertainty.

Mindfulness in Action

Notice what happens within your mind when you are agitated or impatient. Notice how your body reacts as well. This is where your JustBE practices come in handy. Pause whenever you notice you are activated. Breathe mindfully. Maybe you need to walk away from the person or situation for a few moments. Choose a handjam that will help you settle. Experiment with your JustBE skillset to see what helps.

Honor

Take a deep mindful breath and honor yourself by nodding your chin down ever so slightly to your own wise heart and mind. Honor those around you in the same way. You have what it takes to JustBE! Have a mindful day!

21) Labyrinth for Peace

Let's begin by getting into our mindfulness posture.

The handjam for this practice is I AM A WISE BEING.

Instructions: Place your pointer finger at the bottom of the labyrinth where the opening is. Pause here for three breaths. Slowly move your finger between the lines until you get to the center of the labyrinth. Pause here for three breaths. As you breathe out, send the peace that lives inside of you out to the world. Imagine it actually coming out through your breath and filling your space with bountiful peace. You have the ability to bring peace wherever you go. Slowly, follow your finger around to the end of the labyrinth where you began.

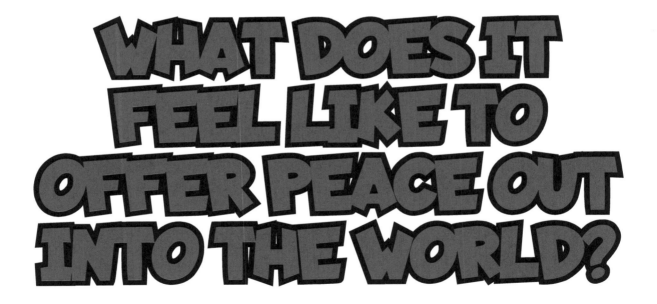

WHAT DOES IT FEEL LIKE TO OFFER PEACE OUT INTO THE WORLD?

START HERE

Handjam

To prepare for the handjam, bring your elbows to your sides (your waist), and let your palms come open. Take a deep inhalation, exhale fully and begin repeating the phrase I AM A WISE BEING (five times aloud, five times silently) while tapping your fingers. Place your left hand over your heart and your right hand over your left. Stay here for 10 mindful breaths. Let's mindfully breathe together.

Wisdom

You always have the choice to offer peace by connecting into the wisdom you have inside your heart. Peace begins with you.

Mindfulness in Action

Bringing awareness to everything you do is a powerful way to bring peace into everyday experiences and open the door to your wise mind. You can make a difference with the words and actions you choose. Take a mindful breath in. As you exhale, allow these words in: "You can make a difference with the words and actions you choose." Pause and take another mindful breath. Sometimes the most powerful way to affect outer change is to create change from within.

Honor

Take a deep mindful breath and honor yourself by nodding your chin down ever so slightly to your own wise heart and mind. Honor those around you in the same way. Have a mindful day!

WHEN DO YOU FEEL WISE? WAS IT SOMETHING YOU SAID, OR MAYBE SOMETHING YOU DID? MAYBE YOU PAUSED WHEN YOU WANTED TO REACT AND INSTEAD WERE ABLE TO RESPOND IN A WISER WAY. DRAW OR WRITE WHAT THIS EXPERIENCE WAS LIKE FOR YOU.

22) Empathy

Come into your mindfulness posture, and practice not thinking about how to begin, but allow your body to lead the way. Your body knows what to do.

The handjam for today is EMPATHY.

Mindfulness

Empathy can be described as "walking in another's shoes." What does it mean to have empathy? By noticing what others are experiencing and feeling, we can build deeper connections with people and the world around us. It's an acknowledgment that even though we may have individual differences, we all go through struggles at one time or another. Recently, while driving, my daughter and I saw a big German shepherd crossing the street. He seemed to be limping and as we got closer we noticed he had three legs. His front left leg was gone. He was smiling and walking the best he could. My daughter and I looked at each other for a moment and then looked back at the dog hobbling along. There was a moment shared in which we wondered what it might feel like to be a dog with three legs and move slowly with a limp. We attuned to each other's feelings and the dog's struggle, and let it soften our hearts. There are many moments during the day to open our eyes to the lives being lived all around us and soften into our hearts and breathe kindness out onto others, including animals. This is empathy. Give yourself a hug! Yes, cross your arms, hug yourself and twist left to right. By learning how to soothe ourselves, we become better at soothing others when the need arises.

Handjam

To prepare for the handjam, bring your elbows to your sides (your waist), and let your palms come open. Take a deep inhalation, exhale fully and begin repeating the phrase EMPATHY (five times aloud, five times silently) while you tap your fingers. Place your left hand over your heart and your right hand over your left. Stay here for 10 mindful breaths. Let's mindfully breathe together.

Wisdom

Many organizations with a mission to help others were founded on the basis of a strong feeling of empathy. The Red Cross, the Humane Society, homeless shelters and orphanages are but a few. "To walk in another's shoes" is a figure of speech used to express what it might feel to be that person and to live the life he or she is living. When our awareness opens to that idea, a feeling of interconnectedness and kindness naturally arises. From there, it becomes almost impossible to impose any kind of harm, because the separateness we once felt falls away. The cool thing about empathy is it grows with awareness and practice. Empathy is medicine for our world.

Mindfulness in Action

Today, take a look at the people (or animals) around you and notice the feelings they are going through. Look into their eyes. JustBE with them and take a closer look. What do you see? Notice how empathy connects you to this other being. The world needs your empathy. Offer a dose whenever you can!

Honor

Take a deep mindful breath and honor yourself by nodding your chin down ever so slightly to your own wise heart and mind. Honor those around you in the same way. Have a mindful day!

23) Kind Self, Kind World

Settle into your mindfulness posture. Notice your jaw. Are you clenching it at all? Allow your jaw to slightly open, so that your face can soften and feel at ease. Stay here for a few seconds and observe how you feel when you bring awareness to your jaw.

Today's handjam is KIND SELF, KIND WORLD.

Mindfulness

We are many things. Sometimes we think we are just this or that: a daughter, son, athlete, jokester, artist, etc. But we are made up of many parts, and examining some of them can help us remember what is good and right within us. Bringing kindness to ourselves brings kindness into the world.

The illustration that goes along with this practice is just one example of the many colorful patterns, shapes and parts of ourselves. Give yourself a moment to take in all the parts that make you YOU.

Handjam

To prepare for the handjam, bring your elbows to your sides (your waist), and let your palms come open. Take a deep inhalation, exhale fully and begin repeating the phrase KIND SELF, KIND WORLD (five times aloud, five times silently) while tapping your fingers. Place your left hand over your heart and your right hand over your left. Stay here for 10 mindful breaths. Let's mindfully breathe together.

Wisdom

Mandalas are circular symmetrical designs that symbolize well-being and can be found in many different cultures throughout history. On page 82, you'll see one example of a Mandala I created. On page 83 there is a blank Mandala for you to design. There are also a few more blank Mandalas on pages 100-102. Coloring Mandalas can help you calm down. Choose one, and then grab a few of your favorite colored pencils or markers. Start coloring the center of your Mandala with the boldest color. Then start to color around the center with some of the softer shades. Practice not thinking too much about what your Mandala will look like in the end; instead, enjoy the process of creating without having a specific goal in mind. Allow the creative part of you to come through, by trusting in what colors you select. The center of the Mandala represents your inner power and boldness. The softer colors represent the softness that you put out into the world through kind words and actions. When you are finished coloring, make a line down the middle of your Mandala.

Fun Fact: Softness does not equal weakness. You can be kind, soft and strong all together. Write or draw all the things you like about yourself on the right side of the line. Be specific. Write characteristics that are not based on what you look like or how you dress. Focus more on things like, "Kind, a good friend, thoughtful, easy to talk with, etc." Next, on the left side of the line, write down, "I am." Then read what each line says, from left to right, starting each sentence with "I am. . . " When you are done, place your Mandala in a special place where you can see it every day.

Mindfulness in Action

Notice what "kind" thoughts come to your mind during your day and why? For example, a friend may help you with something you've dropped, or you might see someone open a door for a person who needs an extra hand. Notice where you were and what happened when these kind thoughts and experiences arose.

This is loving awareness.

Honor

Take a deep mindful breath and honor yourself by nodding your chin down ever so slightly to your own wise heart and mind. Honor those around you in the same way. Have a mindful day!

I AM...

CREATIVE
OPEN-MINDED

FRIENDLY

MINDFUL
A DOG-LOVER

82

24) I Know I Matter

Let's begin our JustBE practice by coming into our mindfulness posture.

Today's handjam is I KNOW I MATTER.

TAP THIGHS

Mindfulness

Consider the word "alone." Now separate it into "Al-One." It's one word that seems to have two meanings, depending on how you see it! How we look at the word "alone" is similar to how we look at our experiences. When you feel alone, it may be helpful to remember that you are part of a greater whole, the same way the word "alone" can be understood as being "Al-One."

Repeat "Al-One, Al-One, Al-One" in your mind while tapping alternate thighs with your hands, palms facing down on top of your thighs. Relax your shoulders back and down, and let your jaw be soft and relaxed as well. Continue for about 30 seconds while mindfully breathing as you tap. The next time you feel "lonely," you can practice this exercise and see what changes. Allow the tapping to soothe you and take you into experiencing the "whole" you.

Handjam

To prepare for the handjam, bring your elbows to your sides (your waist), and let your palms come open. Take a deep inhalation, exhale fully and begin repeating the phrase I KNOW I MATTER (five times aloud, five times silently) while you tap your fingers. Place your left hand over your heart and your right hand over your left. Stay here for 10 mindful breaths. Let's mindfully breathe together.

Wisdom

What is one of your strengths you can think of? Pause. We all have strengths, so choose at least one. What would someone who knows you well say your strength is? This is one of your contributions to this world, so don't forget!

Mindfulness in Action

I learned a mindful walking practice from Thich Nhat Hanh, a meditation teacher, which I'd like to share. As you walk today, imagine a lotus flower blooming under each step you take, creating a magical Mandala-like pattern around your home, school and community. Each step you take is leaving a flower of strength behind you and each step matters. This is mindfulness in action at its best! On the next page, there is an example of a lotus flower with a list of words around it that give me strength. There is also a blank lotus flower for you to design. You can make a copy of it (to use it again in the future), color it in and write down your strengths.

Honor

Take a deep mindful breath and honor yourself by nodding your chin down ever so slightly to your own wise heart and mind. Honor those around you in the same way. Have a mindful day!

LOTUS FLOWER PATH

I BELIEVE IN ME

EMPATHY

COMPASSION

PEACE

INTERCONNECTED

COURAGE

STRENGTH

I MATTER

JUSTBE

KINDNESS

25) Feelings Come and Go

Let's come into our mindfulness posture. Check in with your eyes. Are they sleepy, heavy, wide open? Soften your gaze for a moment by looking a few feet ahead of you at a single point. Focus on this spot with a soft gaze while taking in all that is around you in view. What is it like to have your eyes open, fixed on one point in stillness? Do not judge the thoughts that come in response to this question. Remain curious and breathe into this moment.

Today's handjam is FEELINGS COME AND GO.

Fun Fact: Cloud formations come and go, much like our feelings. Go outside today and look up and check it out.

Mindfulness

Just like clouds appear and disappear and our breath begins and ends, so do feelings come and go. Everything is ever-changing, including our feelings. Of course, it's natural to want to hold onto good feelings and let go of ones that don't feel so good. What if we could flow with change just as cloud formations seem to do so effortlessly? Noticing and observing what we are feeling is a valuable step in gaining awareness. From there, we can choose how we want to relate to these feelings. When we skip over this "observing" step, we may find ourselves "reacting" to our feelings, which is different than "relating" to them. Think of it this way: Sometimes a doctor will check your reflexes by tapping on a point on your knee. Your foot will mysteriously kick up, which is kind of funny, and they call this a "knee jerk reaction." This tells the doctor that your reflexes are working well. Similarly, when you "react" to your feelings in a knee jerk type of way, there is no pause or access to your wise mind. The good news? When you add a sprinkle or two (or ten) of awareness into the moment, you become magically able to respond with a clear mind and a calm heart. The key is to catch yourself before you "react" so that you can choose to "respond" mindfully.

Handjam

To prepare for the handjam, bring your elbows to your sides (your waist), and let your palms come open. Take a deep inhalation, exhale fully and begin repeating the phrase FEELINGS COME AND GO (five times aloud, five times silently) while tapping your fingers.

Place your left hand over your heart and your right hand over your left. Stay here for 10 mindful breaths. Let's mindfully breathe together.

Wisdom

Knowing yourself gives you power. Not the kind of power to *overpower* others, but the kind that adds more peace to our world. How? When you are clear in your mind and know what you need, you find better ways to ask for it and get that need met. It's equally important to understand what you feel when that need does *not* get met. Refer to feelings/needs chart on pages 11-13. Taking some time out to go within, quiet down, listen and JustBE helps you clear away the cobwebs of confusion and arrive at clarity. This takes practice—every day.

Mindfulness in Action

When you notice a feeling that grabs you, pause and start to breathe mindfully. Notice where in your body you have the feeling, and breathe kindness into that place. Notice how long the feeling lasts, and when it lifts and goes away.

Honor

Take a deep, mindful breath and honor yourself by nodding your chin down ever so slightly to your own wise heart and mind. Honor those around you in the same way. Have a mindful day!

26) Interdependence

Settle into your mindfulness posture.

Today's handjam is INTERDEPENDENCE.

Mindfulness

Interdependence isn't a word we come across often, but it's an important one to know: It means understanding how all beings are interconnected, and how we affect one another. On the simplest level, think about the fact that every living thing breathes. It's not something we usually think about, just like we don't think about walking: We just walk. Our breath connects us because we all breathe. It also connects us to nature, because the trees send out oxygen for us and all other animals on earth so that we can keep breathing. Breathe into the simplicity of what connects us. Take three mindful breaths here. When you have time, check out the short film on YouTube "Connected" by Tiffany Shlain.

Handjam

To prepare for the handjam, bring your elbows to your sides (your waist), and let your palms come open. Take a deep inhalation, exhale fully and begin repeating INTERDEPENDENCE (five times aloud, five times silently) while tapping your fingers. Place your left hand over your heart and your right hand over your left. Stay here for 10 mindful breaths. Let's mindfully breathe together.

Wisdom

When we slow down, turn inward, reflect, pause and JustBE, we feel a deeper, more connected place within ourselves and the world around us. Why is this important? Because this is where our wisdom, creativity, open-mindedness and tender heart live. It's just beneath the surface of our skin. It's not far away! But when we are constantly moving and doing stuff, this interconnected place within us can get lost. Yet, once you find and feel this place within you, you know interconnectedness intimately, through the wisdom of your body, and your wise heart.

Mindfulness in Action

We are nearing the end of our JustBE practices, yet we are never truly done with practicing how to JustBE. Remember you can always sprinkle your JustBE skills into your everyday experiences. And you've directly experienced your own JustBE toolkit that is filled with lots of intentions, handjams and other mindfulness techniques that offer a dose of kindness no matter what comes your way. Don't forget that PEACE BEGINS WITH YOU.

Now it's time to share these practices with others. Tag—you're it!

Honor

Take a deep mindful breath and honor yourself by nodding your chin down ever so slightly to your own wise heart and mind. Rest here for a moment. Feel a sense of accomplishment—JustBE. Honor those around you. Have a mindful day!

27) Take What You Need Tabs

"Take what you need" tabs (on page 93) are a fun and simple way to notice what you need, and "take what you need." You can use a tab as a way to help resolve conflict, build awareness of your emotional needs, invite communication with others and develop self-compassion.

Suggested Uses: Give someone a tab as a kind way to tell him or her what you need. For example, you said something that didn't come out the way you had hoped and you want to talk about it and ask for forgiveness. Offering a tab as a way to open up this conversation could be just what is needed. A tab can also offer an opportunity to ask if someone needs a "hug" or "a mindful breath" before a big test or project. Or place one in your pocket for the day as a kind offering for yourself to "slow down," or feel more "gratitude". There is also one empty tab for you to write a need not found on this list.

Instructions: Make a copy of the tabs and cut along the lines. Hang them up at home or at school (or in your break room at the office). Pause before you reach for a tab, and take a mindful breath. Then, gently tear a tab off for yourself or for someone who needs one.

Take what you need...

A mindful breath	Pause	Laughter	Self-compassion	Joy	Optimism	Kindness	Hug	Gratitude	Self-compassion	Forgiveness	Laughter	Hug	Pause	Love	Joy	Gratitude

As a finger labyrinth begins and ends at the same place, I thought it would make sense to end with the intention we began with—"Peace Begins with Me." My wish is that all of the JustBE mindfulness practices have given you an opportunity to know the center of your wise being. From this still point within, you can take your wisdom outward and into your everyday experiences with an expanded sense of awareness, a willingness to feel what you are feeling and a readiness to share the gifts of JustBE-ing. Let's take a breath in, and as we exhale together, let's do the handjam "Peace Begins with Me" together five times aloud and then five times silently. Place your left hand over your heart and your right hand over your left. Stay here for 10 mindful breaths. Let's mindfully breathe together.

Honor

Honor yourself, and honor each other. Remember, Peace Begins with You!!!

On the opposite page is an example of how you can bring peace into our world. Express how YOU want to bring more peace into the world on page 96.

PEACE BEGINS WITH ME

WHEN DO I FEEL PEACE?
I FEEL AT PEACE IN MY HOME

WHAT DO I LOOK LIKE WHEN I'M PEACEFUL?

HOW CAN YOU OFFER PEACE TO OUR WORLD?

RECYCLING

HOW DOES BEING PEACEFUL HELP OUR WORLD?

IT HELPS OUR WORLD BY LEAVING A BIT OF PEACE WITH WHOEVER I'M WITH AND WHEREVER I GO

PEACE BEGINS WITH ME

WHEN DO I FEEL PEACE?	WHAT DO I LOOK LIKE WHEN I'M PEACEFUL?
HOW CAN YOU OFFER PEACE TO OUR WORLD?	HOW DOES BEING PEACEFUL HELP OUR WORLD?

You have completed the **JustBE** program and earned a JustBE certificate.

Fill in your name and put your certificate up at home or at school to remind you to practice JustBE-ing.

Congrats

JustBE Graduate!!!

I, _____, have successfully completed the JustBE program! I have learned JustBE mindfulness skills to create peace, calm, stillness, awareness, self-compassion and empathy. I will practice these skills every day and offer them to others, so they will strengthen and spread into my community.

REFLECTIONS

HOW DOES LENGTHENING YOUR EXHALE HELP TO RELAX YOUR BODY? DRAW OR WRITE YOUR ANSWER.

REFLECTIONS

REMEMBER, JUST LIKE THE BOTTOM OF THE OCEAN REMAINS CALM DESPITE A STORM ABOVE THE SURFACE, YOU ALSO HAVE A PLACE OF DEEP CALM INSIDE OF YOU, NO MATTER WHAT'S GOING ON AROUND YOU. DRAW OR WRITE DOWN WHAT YOU LOOK AND FEEL LIKE WHEN YOU EXPERIENCE THIS CALM PLACE WITHIN.

REFLECTIONS

WHO DO YOU WANT TO SHARE A HANDJAM WITH AND WHY? HOW WILL IT HELP THIS PERSON? DRAW A PICTURE OR DESCRIBE THIS IN WORDS.

REFLECTIONS

HOW HAS BECOMING MORE AWARE HELPED YOU IN SCHOOL, AT HOME OR WITH FRIENDS? DRAW A PICTURE OR WRITE YOUR ANSWER.

REFLECTIONS

WHICH HANDJAM IS YOUR FAVORITE? HOW HAS IT HELPED YOU? WHO WOULD YOU LIKE TO SHARE IT WITH AND WHY? DRAW A PICTURE OR DESCRIBE THIS IN WORDS.

REFLECTIONS

WHAT DOES MY FACE AND BODY LANGUAGE LOOK LIKE WHEN I PAUSE AND SPEAK MINDFULLY? DRAW A PICTURE OR DESCRIBE IT IN WORDS.